THE LAST DAY'S ARMY for KIDS

This ARMY will surprise you!

BJ Jenkins

Illustrated by BJ Jenkins and Alicia Estis

Presented to:

_____

By:

_____

Date:

_____

The Last Day's Army for Kids by BJ Jenkins

Illustrated by BJ Jenkins and Alicia Estis

Copyright © 2022 BJ Jenkins

ISBN 978-1-953229-31-1

Special Thanks:

To the Holy Spirit, who inspired the idea
and every word of this book, helping me to
make the deep things of God simple.

To Alicia Estis for her dedication
in editing this book.

And it shall come to pass
That whoever calls
on the name of the Lord
Shall be saved.
For in Mount Zion
and in Jerusalem there shall
be deliverance,
As the Lord has said,
Among **the remnant** whom
the Lord calls.

Joel 2:32

The King is Coming!

He's coming soon!

We MUST prepare for war.

The enemy will rise to fight

like we've never seen before.

God is calling

and preparing

an army soon arising.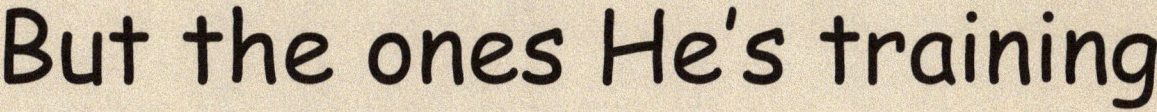

But the ones He's training

for the fight,

you'll find a bit SURPRISING!

God has CHOSEN

for this time

the children and the youth.

They'll lead the remnant

of the Church,

in Spirit and in Truth.

All the children

and the youth

prepare now prayerfully.

Parents, get your babies ready.

This is their **DESTINY!**

When children see

an evil spirit,

they will not be afraid.

They'll tell it to just

"GO AWAY,"

all in Jesus' name!

All the youth,

prepare yourself,

ages three to twenty-nine,

to prophesy and see visions,

and to do it ALL the time!

Faith will make it possible

for your spiritual eyes to see

the visions God will give to you

when you trust Him

and BELIEVE.

God will speak directly through

your youthful generation

as YOU prophesy to people

in every tongue and nation!

The weapons you will use

will be DIFFERENT

for this war,

for they are supernatural

like you've never seen before.

Your sword will be

the WORD of God

and appear at your demand.

It will cut the enemy in half

as it springs forth

from your hand.

The angel armies

of the Lord

will fight along YOUR side.

They will lead you

to the enemy

when it tries to hide.

EVERYTHING

you'll need to fight,

God will give to you.

With the

Seven Horns anointing,

He will pour out on you, too!

In this very intense war,

some will even die.

But they will win a

GREAT reward,

so we should never cry!

They will wear a robe that's

lined with red and

will have a different crown.

They will live with

the great martyrs

in a SPECIAL part of town.

Fighting with the Remnant
will be the GREATEST call.

Will you stand and

fight with God?

Will you give your all?

If you say yes,

NOW is the time

you must prepare to start.

Pray for the Holy Spirit

to purify your heart.

YOU are the generation

He has chosen for this reason

because the

Kingdom of our God

will come this very season!

THE
END

BJ Jenkins Ministries

Children's Author • Children's Minister • Speaker

All BOOK Titles offer these options!

Rhyming Book

Rhyming Book—These fun children's rhyming books are illustrated in full color and measure 8 1/2" x 8 1/2". They are easy to read and teach the deep things of God in a simple way even a child can understand. These books are also a great introduction to the curriculum. For Kids Pre-school and Up

Curriculum

Learning Curriculum—These books are printed in full color and measure 8 1/2" x 11". They contain full lesson plans complete with lessons, exercises, games, and even use a puppet to encourage the children. These lessons do not require any advance preparation or study and are designed to be read straight from the pages. For Kids K-12 (and even adults)

Prayer Journal

Prayer Journal—These books are full color and measure 6" x 9". This is a companion to the curriculum. The children are encouraged to journal during each lesson and record what they hear the Lord saying to them. Each lesson has a memory verse, important things to remember, a place to draw pictures, and plenty of room to journal their thoughts. At the end of each chapter, there is a prayer or exercise for the children that will help re-enforce each subject. For Kids K-12

Puppets & Music

Each series also offers a unique puppet that is used along with the curriculum to introduce each lesson. We also offer a CD with music and character voices.

Teach the deeper things of God. They're not too young to start,
for their childlike faith will open the windows of their heart.

bjjenkinsministries.com

bjjenkinsministries@gmail.com

The NOT Series by BJ Jenkins

The NOT Series, by BJ Jenkins, is a series of books that teach subjects such as the Fruit of the Spirit, Prayer, Hearing the Voice of God, what will be happening in these Last Days, and the story of Jesus.

These books are available as a Rhyming Book, Curriculum, and as a Prayer Journal.

Each series also offers a unique puppet that is used along with the curriculum to introduce each lesson. We also offer a CD with music and character voices.

Hi, I'm Miss Molly.

Based on the Best Selling Books
by Sadhu Sundar Selvaraj

These 8 1/2" x 8 1/2" books teach subjects like: What happens when we wait on God, how to hear God's voice, the proper way to pray, the 9 gifts of the Spirit, how to have your spiritual eyes opened, how to be translated in the Spirit, The 7 Horns anointing, and the powers of the age to come.

Hardback Rhyming Books Available at
bjjenkinsministries.com

These books are also available as a Rhyming Book, Curriculum, and as a Prayer Journal
for E-BOOK ONLY at www.jesusministries.com

CPSIA information can be obtained
at www.ICGtesting.com
Printed in the USA
BVHW021140030422
633070BV00002B/15